Col

An Alternative View

Colin Buchanan

Bishop of Woolwich

Mark Earey

Team Rector of Morley, West Yorkshire

Gilly Myers

Succentor, Sacrist and Minor Canon of Durham Cathedral

Tim Stratford

Vicar of the Church of the Good Shepherd, West Derby, Liverpool

GROVE BOOKS LIMITED
RIDLEY HALL RD CAMBRIDGE CB3 9HU

Contents

Acknowledgments

The authors gratefully acknowledge the encouragement of the Group for the Renewal of Worship and thank, in particular, James Steven and Anne de Lange for comments and suggestions on the early draft of this booklet.

The Cover Illustration is by Peter Ashton

First Impression August 2002
ISSN 0144-1728
ISBN 1 85174 505 X

Introduction

1

The Church of England encounters its modern (and some traditional language) collects in the part of Common Worship first published in 1997 as 'Calendar, Lectionary and Collects.'

These Common Worship collects saw the light of day well before most of the other liturgical texts had been agreed. We shall see a little later the rationale that created them, but here we observe that they quite quickly ran into trouble over their language. Once in use, they were widely resisted on the grounds that they had too much of a Tudor (or BCP) 'feel' to them—a characteristic originating in particular persons on the Liturgical Commission, but not really picked up or scrutinized sufficiently closely by the Synod in the process of amending and authorizing them. The sheer fact that they were authorized early in the Common Worship process meant that criticism could be registered and taken on board at a point long prior to any reasoned critique of, say, the eucharistic prayers. Sure enough, Wakefield diocese passed a diocesan synod motion and brought it to General Synod in July 2001:

> 'That this Synod, in the light of criticisms of the new collects for Common Worship, request the House of Bishops to commission additional collects for each Sunday and Feast Day in the Liturgical Year in a worthy contemporary idiom.'

This was passed overwhelmingly by the General Synod, and the House of Bishops duly instructed the Liturgical Commission. The Commission in turn asked Paul Roberts to lead a sub-group to address the motion—and in Autumn 2001 the sub-group put out a questionnaire (and published the results from it), with a view to providing a new set of collects as requested by Synod.

The present booklet is intended as a contribution to the debate which has been bubbling in the church since the new collects came into use and which has now come to a head. We are suggesting not primarily a new set of texts (though we do offer some by way of example) but a new approach to the use of collects which, we believe, has more connection with the reality of the Church of England today, and is more likely to rescue the collect as a useful form of prayer than the simple provision of a full alternative set of texts.

2

How Did We Get Here?

This chapter explores underlying principles which bear upon any treatment of collects, with a little history along the way.

The Origins of the Term

Martin Dudley, in his scholarly Alcuin Monograph on Anglican collects, opens up several different possibilities as to how a form of prayer gained the unlikely title of 'collect.'[1] There are two leading candidates:

- the (Gallican) notion that it concludes a section of prayers, summarizing or 'collect'-ing them;

- the (Roman) notion that the 'collect'-ing is gathering the people, rather than the prayers, so it is an opening prayer to begin a liturgy.

Purists of either sort are therefore able to proclaim that the origins demonstrate that a collect is a prayer which must perform exactly this (or the other) function. Sensible people will remember that etymology (or linguistic origins) provide a wholly unreliable basis for determining present meaning. What would we say, for instance, to a plumber who came to repair our pipes insisting—from his 'plumb' stem title—he must use lead in them? The key to the concept of a collect will be found to lie much more in its internal form than in its external location and relationships.

The Classic Form

Whilst there are strong biblical roots to the theological shape of a collect, the precise criteria which may be applied to its purest linguistic form derive very clearly from the Latin language collects of Rome in the fifth and sixth centuries. This terseness and precision were brilliantly preserved by Cranmer's translations and adaptations, and thus became a recognized literary form among prayers in the English language. The analysis of the form provides the following five sections, which is exemplified by the collect of the sixth Sunday after Trinity in the 1549 BCP:

1. The address: the classic vocative.

'God…'

2. The relative clause in the second person singular (or 'appositional phrase'), attributing God's nature, powers or past action to him. This is a principle broadly based in the Psalms and in prayers like that of Jeremiah (Jer 32). It does what uninformed prejudice often derides nowadays—telling God things he already knows—but does so for theological reasons.

'…which hast prepared for them that love thee such good things as pass all man's understanding…'

3. The petition—the central (and often the only) imperative in the prayer. In the classic form this is dependent in its content upon the attributes of God set out in section 2. It is the immediate need that is named here, and the longer-term need is located in section 4.

'…pour into our hearts such love toward thee…'

4. The aspiration or end-purpose of the petition, setting out an ultimate concern for God's purposes, kingdom and glory, rather than simply ending upon our need.

'…that we, loving thee in all things, may obtain thy promises which exceed all that we can desire…'

5. The mediation, as in all prayers. A further ascription may follow the mention of Jesus as shown opposite [not in 1549 text].

'…through Jesus Christ our Lord.' ['…who liveth and reigneth with thee and the Holy Ghost, ever one God, world without end.']

Not all features are present in all collects, but the structural outline is sufficient to allow us to define what a collect is and to recognize one when we see it. It also gives broad parameters to rash souls who would write modern collects. It is unclear at what point a prayer through sheer length ceases to be a collect. Cranmer wrote long collects of Advent Sundays, and in 1552 called the 'Prayer of St Chrysostom' a collect (though later generations called it the Prayer of St Chrysostom). But an element of conciseness is widely understood as integral to this form of prayer.

Cranmer in general cut down what had been a complexity of rules about collects. He allowed but one collect of each Sunday or Feast Day, though in

Communion there was also a collect 'for the king.' He had no problems in calling the opening prayer for purity a 'collect,' and he equally did not mind placing at the end of 1549 a set of *Collects to be said after the offertory, when there is no Communion...*' which suggests he was not bothered by origins. In 1552 these closing collects could also be said after the collects of Morning or Evening Prayer.

In short Cranmer was given both to tightly constructed classic collects, and to other somewhat longer and more flexible ones. He was, of course, concerned for biblical doctrine,[2] but seems to have been untroubled by location, and unbothered by the idea of several collects in a service for different reasons, though only one would be 'of' that day. There were two additional ones—of some fame—on Good Friday. The idea of a seasonal collect—of Lent or Advent—additional to the collect of the day (an idea which is of interest to the compilers of this booklet), is a 1662 addition.

When the moderns have found themselves handling Cranmer's work, they have tended to emphasize that *the* collect, the sole collect 'of' the day, should stand alone. On the other hand the beauty, brevity, and relative antiquity of the form have always mesmerized Anglicans a bit, and they have learned collects by heart (a health-giving if slightly dated exercise) and been sure they knew what a collect was and what it was *for*. The present writers are marginally less doctrinaire about either the form or the role of a collect, but happily here try to meet the programme of those who are sure.

A Note On Terminology
Note that the collect appropriate for a particular day is the collect 'of' that day. The petition 'for' which the prayer is offered (section 3 in the tabulated analysis above) is by definition something or somebody on behalf of which or whom we are praying—thus in 1549 the second collect is 'for the king.' Similarly in 1662 Morning Prayer we have the rubric:

'Then shall follow three Collects: The first *of* the day: The second *for* Peace: the Third *for* Aid against all Perils...'

Those who ignore this ground rule and pray, for example, 'The collect for Christmas Day' are in grave danger of finding themselves similarly announcing 'The collect for the Conversion of St Paul' or (worse) 'The collect for the beheading of John the Baptist.' We do well to be purists here; and, though the *Prayer Book* will allow itself that a collect is 'appointed for' a certain day, it then becomes the collect 'of' that day.

Addressing God As 'You'

Before we approach the present day, we recall that we now address God as 'you,' and, where Cranmer and 1662 are much loved, we need to offer one small footnote on trans-cultural usage of those collects.

The second person singular relative clause goes well in Tudor (or 'traditional') English—'God, which hast...' (or 'Our Father, which art...'). It does not work in modern (or 'contemporary') English—try 'O God, who have....' Nor will it go into the third person ('O God, who has...')—though the Welsh tried this with traditional English, and spectacularly erroneous results, in 1984. An artifice is needed, and one of the two following may be helpful:

(a) A past tense in the relative clause ('O God, who made the heavens...')

(b) A cunning use of a genuinely third person relative ('O God, by whose power the world was created...')

The Rationale of the Collect

The conventional wisdom of today's Liturgical Commission is that the collect arose as a form of prayer to bring the people together (or 'collect' them) into public worship, and its place was accordingly at the beginning of a rite. Such a prayer might be of a general sort, without particular theme or focus, so long as it fulfilled the 'gathering' function—presumably by being fairly short and not too specific in content.

However, it has been inevitable that at high seasons (Christmas, Easter, Saints' Days, baptism, ordination) some mention of the occasion should figure within the collect, so that the 1662 BCP provided a set of collects of most Sundays in the year of a wholly general sort, and some which highlighted the theme of the day. They were set out in 1662 with the epistles and gospels of the day, and had a very clear look of belonging to them. But in the 1552 communion the collect of the day had *preceded* the collect for the king; and it is possible that the order was reversed in 1662 for mere convenience—that is, that the change meant that, when the officiant had once turned to the collects, epistles and gospels, he could now read all three in sequence without turning back.

It is thus not surprising that the sense that a collect has a direct relation to a Sunday theme has been 'around.' A variant on this arises from Cranmer's collect of Advent 2—the collect occasioned by a phrase in the Epistle (Romans 15) which is actually not a main advent theme, but as a collect gave rise to 'Bible Sunday.' So when the two-year lectionary was produced by the ecumenical Joint Liturgical Group (JLG) in 1968, and became part of (draft)

Series 3 communion in 1971, the underlying themes of each Sunday became of some moment. Thus the quest was soon on for collects which were not only in 'you' form, but also related to the lectionary themes. The Group for Renewal of Worship (then still named Latimer House Liturgy Group) rose triumphantly to the occasion and published a set of collects (by P Akehurst and A Bishop) in late 1972, in a handy 'reading desk' format, ready for use when Series 3 was authorized.[3] The set went through four editions and had lasted five years in pirate use before official collects came along. It had an unsurprising 'instant' look to it, and few of those collects have survived into current use—but it marvellously assisted the theme of each Sunday, and fixed the association of the collect with the readings.

In formal terms this association never became a union. The collect remained formally at the end of the Preparation, whilst the readings became the substance of the Ministry of the Word—and this distinction has been the clearer where congregations have remained standing through the Preparation but have then sat after the collect in order to hear the first reading. However, the use of 'thematic' collects, related to the readings, throughout the ASB era gave to many the idea that the collect was not so much a closing of the Preparation but a way of introducing a theme, shortly to be spelt out in readings and sermon. In many churches the collect came to be explained (both orally and on printed service sheets) as the 'theme prayer.'

In Common Worship, the introduction of the three-year lectionary (which is not thematically based, but at root arises from semi-continuous reading of Scripture) meant that the ASB pattern could be, and perhaps needed to be, abandoned. After that, the only principles the Liturgical Commission could follow seem to have been:

i) except at high seasons, we have no indication what the contents of the collect of the day should be;

ii) so we might as well simply pick up the BCP collects (which have been all too summarily dumped in the ASB) and relate them to the same Sundays;

iii) these BCP collects have a stained-glass window beauty to them, and that needs conserving also.

Thus the CW collects arose. They did so, not as a solely English work, but in collaboration with liturgists from the Anglican churches in Scotland, Wales and Ireland.

The New Task

The response in General Synod to the Wakefield indictment of the CW collects was highly supportive, including Michael Perham in penitent mode. But the issue is now what should be supplied to meet the General Synod resolution? Is there a principle (apart from the Wakefield desire to be more contemporary) which would indicate how to write a coherent set? The Irish collection (to go with the three-year lectionary) has recently been reviewed in *News of Liturgy*;[4] and many have commended the very interesting *Opening Prayers: Collects in Contemporary Language* (Canterbury Press, 1999)[5] produced by the Roman Catholic Church's International Commission on English in the Liturgy (ICEL).

There is a further interesting question as to how to authorize new collects. Should the rubric in Communion be changed (by full Revision Committee process?) so that other collects can be used without being combed over individually? Or should a new collect-ion go for treatment line by line in General Synod? Or should we follow the pattern set by the illegal use of the Akehurst-Bishop collects for five years? We do not, in this booklet, attempt an answer to such legal imponderables—but we do have a suggestion to make about what sort of prayers it would be sensible for the church to authorize.

3 A Sense of Direction?

We have looked at the structure and purpose of the collect, given a brief history of its use in the Church of England and glanced at the policy that seems to lie behind the Common Worship collects.

We now examine further the way in which the collect has been used in the Church of England. More specifically, since the notes and rubrics are every bit as important as the liturgical texts themselves, we turn to look at these as they refer to the collect.

Book of Common Prayer

The *Book of Common Prayer* takes for granted that any collect printed under the title of any particular day, is the one to be used on that day at Holy Communion, and Morning and Evening Prayer.

What is explicit is that the collect of a Sunday is also to be used on the days of the following week (and usually the evening before the Sunday—subject to certain logical exceptions). This rule is only overridden when other provision is made, or on the days that follow Christmas Day, Ash Wednesday and Ascension Day. Days on which 'other provision is made' would include, of course, Christmas Day, Ash Wednesday and Ascension Day themselves.

In addition, there are certain times of the year when two collects are to be used, one after the other. On every day in Lent, for example, the collect of Ash Wednesday is to be read after the appointed collect of the day.

> Almighty and everlasting God, who hatest nothing that thou hast made, and dost forgive the sins of all them that are penitent: Create and make in us new and contrite hearts, that we worthily lamenting our sins, and acknowledging our wretchedness, may obtain of thee, the God of all mercy, perfect remission and forgiveness; through Jesus Christ our Lord. Amen.
>
> *Collect for Ash Wednesday*

Thus this collect is given the function of being a seasonal theme prayer. The same is true of the collect of the First Sunday in Advent, which is repeated every day in Advent until Christmas Eve, along with the collect appointed for the day. The collect of the Nativity (Christmas Day) was also to be said daily between Christmas and New Year's Eve, following the collects of the other special days that occur during that period.

The Alternative Service Book

The rules regarding the use of collects remained fairly strict in the ASB, declaring that on seasonal Sundays and all the key Festivals and Holy Days the readings 'and all else which is proper to the service…are said on their appointed days and are not replaced by the service of any other days' unless the provision is subject to a transference, or similar exception.[6]

As in the BCP, a Sunday collect was to be used on the following weekdays, unless there was other official provision.[7]

Beyond these regulations, there were a few significant changes in evidence from the BCP usage.

- The first was that whenever more than one collect was provided, only one collect *need* be used.[8] (Occasionally, more than one collect was provided for a particular day—the days in Easter week, for example.)

- Another rule determined that if a baptism, confirmation, ordination or marriage took place on any of the listed Sundays, Festivals or Holy Days, then the collect of the day had to be used, unless the bishop should direct otherwise.[9]

- A further, significant, difference was that the 'theme' collect, running throughout a season alongside the weekly collects, had slipped quietly away, with no suggestion that the Advent, Christmas or Lent collects should be used beyond the days on which they were appointed.

A Service of the Word 1993

The authorization of A Service of the Word was a turning point in Church of England liturgy for many reasons, and the collect did not go untouched by this revolution. The thematic approach of the ASB collects that sat alongside the JLG two-year lectionary had prepared the way for the line taken in the new service, which said

> 'The collect does not need to be that of the day; it may be a thematic one based on the readings [at the end of the Preparation], or be used to sum up the prayers [in the 'Prayers' section of the service].'
>
> *Introduction to A Service of the Word 1993*

The door had been opened wide for the collect at a main Sunday service to be locally composed, or taken from sources other than the sets on offer in the *Book of Common Prayer* and the *Alternative Service Book*.

The principle and practice of a common collect being used around the whole country on any particular day or occasion had already been diluted by the fact that in each church there was a choice between Prayer Book and ASB collects. These collects differed not only in the sort of language used (contemporary or traditional) but in the content of the prayers themselves. That principle and practice seemed now to have reached breaking point and was about to be strained yet further by the collects provided in Common Worship.

Early Signs in Common Worship

In 1997 the first batch of Common Worship provisions to graduate, fully authorized from the synodical process, was contained in *The Christian Year: Calendar, Lectionary and Collects*. We refer below to the Rules and Notes from this book (which have been transferred into the main Common Worship volume), and to its very useful commentary.

Here are some of the key Common Worship points regarding collects:

- *How many?* Normally on any occasion only one collect is said.[10]

- *Weekdays* The collect for each Sunday is used on the following weekdays, except where other provision is made.[11] (Presumably this applies both to Communion and other services, as in the past. It does not specifically say otherwise.)

- *The seasonal prayer pops up its head once again* Though there is no provision for any of the *collects* to run through a season, the idea has reappeared in relation to the *post-communion prayers*. The collect of the First Sunday of Advent, for example, can be used as a post-communion prayer on any day from the Second Sunday of Advent until Christmas Eve. Similarly, the Ash Wednesday collect can be used as the post-communion prayer on any day from the following Sunday until the day before the Fourth Sunday of Lent.[12]

- *Not linked to readings or themes* 'The collect is fundamentally a "collecting prayer"...As such, though it may often be seasonal, it will not be thematic, and is not essentially a part of the Ministry of the Word or linked with the lections.'[13] Note that the term 'seasonal' in this context means a collect having a seasonal theme, rather than being one which is used throughout a season.

- *A universal principle* 'On as many days as possible, it seems desirable that Anglicans should be using the same collect, even if in slightly differing versions to accommodate the desire for both traditional and contemporary translations.' [14]

This final point makes clear that one of the aims of the Common Worship collects was to unite the Church of England again (!?) around one set of collects. It was hoped that the CW collects would prove to be traditional enough to be used with a Prayer Book congregation (in either their original or 'traditional language' versions), whilst contemporary enough to be used in modern language services. It is therefore ironic (to say the least) that the revolt that has followed their use has probably divided the Church of England more than ever it was in the days of ASB versus BCP collects. Anecdotal evidence suggests that in a large number of Church of England places of worship, each presiding minister does as he or she sees fit, choosing, amending replacing and composing collect prayers week by week and often with no particular consistency of approach.

Service of the Word in Common Worship

The recipe for A Service of the Word—an outline structure plus a set of notes—and its flexibility made it a great success in many contexts. Its potential was further developed in the preparation of Common Worship. The service was adapted so that it could also be the basis of any non-eucharistic weekday service, and the provision for a Service of the Word with a celebration of Holy Communion was sharpened up.

The introductory note about collects, quoted opposite from the 1993 prototype, remained more or less the same. But the guidelines for A Service of the Word with a Celebration of Holy Communion were made more explicit.

Among the changes to the 1993 version of A Service of the Word with Holy Communion was the appearance of a red asterisk by every element of the service which required an authorized text. The collect in a non-Communion context does not have to be an authorized prayer, whereas it does in A Service of the Word with Holy Communion. As a consequence, while there remains tremendous freedom of choice when the service is not Communion, a collect from either the BCP or the Common Worship collection has to be used when there is Communion.

So far, so clear. However, some question of interpretation remains on whether the authorized collect has to be the one appointed to that particular day. Is it significant that the description in the service outline lists 'a collect' rather than 'the collect' (which would be less ambiguous)? There is a note saying that the readings of the day are usually used on Sundays and Principal Holy Days at A Service of the Word with Holy Communion—but this note does not include anything about any other 'propers' that might be associated with the day.

The idea of praying a common collect has certainly not been reclaimed by these adjustments.

Daily Prayer

Daily Prayer has been the most recent addition to the library of Common Worship books. Containing a large collection of prayers and collects for the church's year, it should enrich the church's daily prayer and provide a valuable resource for other acts of worship, too. But it is interesting to consider how the Daily Office Group of the Liturgical Commission, which compiled *Common Worship: Daily Prayer*, have approached the choice of collects. First, we note that

- all the Common Worship collects are printed out in *Common Worship: Daily Prayer*
- in every version of Prayer During the Day, Morning Prayer and Evening Prayer the rubric reads, 'The Collect of the day or the following prayer is said.' Similarly, in Night Prayer each day of the week is provided with a night-themed collect.[15]

Beyond this, anything goes, as far as the collect is concerned! In every service a collect is printed out, which can be used instead of the collect of the day. Indeed, it is fairly *likely* to be used, since it saves turning to another page in the collects section. Prayers for the collect 'slot' are drawn from many sources. They include old favourites, like the Prayer of Richard of Chichester, and contemporary versions of BCP prayers. Some are for mornings, others for evenings. Some are authorized Common Worship collects.

If, during ordinary time, you pray four times on each weekday (Morning Prayer, Prayer During the Day at midday, Evening Prayer and Night Prayer), you could end up saying 24 different collects in the course of a week—and that is before you get to Sunday!

In seasonal time it is a bit different. There are just three different collects in a day (morning and evening prayer share the same one), and the same set is used throughout the whole season. What is more, the seasonal collects for Morning and Evening Prayer are drawn from the Common Worship collects in such a way that a 'key' collect from a Sunday, Principle Feast or Holy Day becomes the prayer for the whole season.

It has to be remembered that *Daily Prayer* is, essentially, a set of worked out versions of A Service of the Word for weekday use, and that users are at liberty to devise their own versions, which may look fairly different from this. Nevertheless, what has been produced by the Liturgical Commission is bound to be understood as having a stamp of authority on it, and we would expect the provision to present the recommended practice.

Daily Prayer does not contradict any of the principles of A Service of the Word—in fact, it interprets the essence of A Service of the Word in a variety of creative ways. The variety of material may well be considered one of the strengths of the provision—a wealth of prayers, gathered together from throughout the Christian centuries. But the following questions still arise:

- What has happened to the principle of the Sunday collect being used throughout the following week (since the other printed collects encourage us not to use the Sunday ones—or, at least, make it easier not to)?
- Has the optimistic principle that a common collect would be used (largely) all around the whole nation on any particular day gone out of the window?

Where Have We Got To?

So far we have discovered a number of different understandings of what is meant when we talk about a 'collect.' Someone speaking of 'collects' could have any, or several, of the following in their mind:

- Prayers of a particular form.
- Prayers which are short and concise—as, for instance, the term is used in Prayer Book Morning and Evening Prayer.
- Prayers that 'collect' the congregation and their prayers— exemplified by their use at the end of the Gathering in the CW Communion. It may or may not need to follow the classic form in order to do this.

- Prayers that 'collect' (in the sense of conclude and summarize) a series of prayers or biddings. They might act in this way as part of the intercessions in A Service of the Word. Equally a series of 'collect-form' prayers might be used to conclude periods of silence following biddings during the intercessions.

- Prayers that 'collect' together the nation or a denomination. This sense of the collect as a 'common' prayer, said in every church on a particular day is strongly present among those who lament the loss of the *Prayer Book* collects.

- Prayers that 'collect' or hold together the theme of the service or one or more of the Bible readings. This is how they became seen in the ASB and how they are designed in *Opening Prayers*.[16]

In the midst of all of this, a new set of collects from the Liturgical Commission is in the melting pot. The next chapter makes some suggestions about what is needed by way of collect provision for the Church of England's future.

Where Do We Go From Here?

4

Whatever the argument for the pattern of collects as the Church of England has inherited them, it may be that the time for a large corpus of weekly one-size-fits-all collects is over.

Gone is the nation's memory for the ways the collects connect with their associated point of the year. It may never have really existed in the first place, though the clergy and some core church members might have possessed it. Is it really sensible to suggest that a prayer which bridges the gap between 'The Gathering' and 'The Liturgy of the Word' in the mid-Epiphany Sunday morning Communion of a church immersed in the direction of the Lectionary is also the most appropriate call to prayer for a small group gathering for Morning Prayer on the following Thursday? The idea that it might be sensible stems from the vain hope that the collects remain important to the spiritual formation of the nation at large. But if the prayer sounds irrelevant, it is of no use to anybody's spiritual formation.

Although Common Worship generally presents the collect of the day as a universal tool it does seem implicitly to accept that this is not necessarily the best way forward in all situations. So its liturgies for Weddings, Funerals, and even Holy Baptism have collects printed within them that can be used instead of the collect of the day. These connect better with the expectations of those who have come to the church, not through a regular discipline of worship all year round, but just for the one occasion. In addition, as we have already seen, the official provision is not crystal clear about how the collect will be chosen when it comes to services governed by A Service of the Word. Furthermore, the purpose of a prayer before 'The Conclusion' or as part of the prayers of intercession (in either of which positions it might be placed in A Service of the Word) must be different to one that follows 'The Gathering.'

CW seems to accept that the collect of the day as a universal tool is not necessarily the best way forward

So what is the point in the Church retaining a set of prayers, one for each week of the year, with the partial expectation that these be used in every service in the week (except where holy days intervene)? Such an idea can only make sense in the context of the Cranmerian aspiration to build a Christian nation through the common formation of a unified liturgy. Undoubtedly this strategy is an important aspect of the Church of England's heritage, but the world has changed and new strategies are needed.

From Weekly to Seasonal?

Amongst all of the Prayer Book collects that are likely to be remembered, two stand out—Advent 1 and Lent 1. No doubt this is because they were used repeatedly over a number of Sundays in many places. As we saw in the last chapter, Common Worship does not allow for such a practice with collects, even though it does allow a similar approach with post-communion prayers. We suggest that the purpose collects are intended to serve, the movement in worship they are supposed to encourage, could be better facilitated by prayers that are used often enough to become familiar—prayers that carry echoes through a *season* rather than a *week*.

There are seventy contemporary language 'collects of the day' for Sundays and principal festivals in the CW Collection. It might be that the church would better be served by seven: Advent; Christmas; Epiphany; 'winter'; Lent; Easter; and 'summer.' It might well be argued that the long period of 'Ordinary Time' reaching into autumn merits provision of more than one collect—but surely a far cry from seventy. A compact collection of collects such as this would present the Church with a real opportunity to distil the essentials of salvation history into a much more manageable 'knapsack' than the present weighty load.

Collects could become, once again, memorable and therefore useful as 'prayers of the heart'

Our contention is that by reducing the number of collects in this way it would be possible for them to become, once again, memorable by at least some of the regular congregation, and therefore useful as 'prayers of the heart'—the sort of memorable corpus of prayers that old romantic notions of the collects have looked for longingly. Part of the reason that the compilers of the CW collects opted for a one-year cycle, rather than a three-year cycle to complement the lectionary, was out of a desire to have the collects 'come round again' more quickly, to aid memorization. The reality is that in most congregations today, 'regular' worshippers might be present only once or twice a month. For most worshippers, even with an annual cycle of prayers, most collects would be encountered much less frequently than annually. By contrast, a single collect for, say, the whole season of Lent, is likely to be encountered two or three times every year, even by those who do not worship weekly. This pattern of 'seasonal stability' coupled with variety over the course of a year is already proving to be a successful way of introducing some of the other variety that Common Worship provides—such as Eucharistic Prayers and forms of confession—to congregations. Why not apply the same approach to collects? A further advantage of this 'seasonal' approach is that it takes the pressure off the questions about language, poetry, richness and complexity. There are, then, two related problems with the CW collects as currently experienced:

- They are only encountered once a year (if that) and so it takes a long time for the poetry, complexity and resonances to become familiar enough to yield their richness.

- They are encountered only aurally, except by the person reading them out. For most in the congregation they pass the ear too quickly even to enter the mind and be comprehensible, let alone do any deeper work. Some churches print out the collect each week on the notice sheet, and this may help but it is by no means universal.

Seasonal collects would get more than one chance to be heard by all and could be printed in the seasonal order of service, where they can be encountered visually as well as aurally by everyone (or, at least, everyone who is able to read). And they are then well placed to be used as a congregational text if that is appropriate. All of this means that even a complex prayer stands a good chance of becoming known and appreciated for what it can offer.

A Lectionary-based Approach?

A different approach is to suggest that collects should carry the resonances of the lectionary. Consequently the area of theological landscape to be covered, and its complexity, are of a different order. The 'Opening Prayers' produced by the Roman Catholic International Commission on English in the Liturgy (ICEL)[17] take this approach and the result is *three* collects for each Sunday and Festival—one for each of the three years of the lectionary. In the Anglican Communion, *A Prayer Book for Australia* (1995)[18] took a similar approach, providing three collects on each Sunday, one for each year of the lectionary. Recognizing that these prayers might not be appropriate at other services on the Sunday or at services during the rest of the week (when the readings would be different) it also provides a 'Prayer for the Week,' which is more general. (And, we might note, it also provides for a 'Prayer for the Season' for Advent and Lent!) The case for this seems a far cry away from the simple need for prayers that help people gird themselves to move from gathering together to listening to God or from sacrament to action. It has been a tempting route for some in the Church of England, as we have wrestled with a new lectionary and found resources such as these coming to hand—but it is not a route that we are recommending.

Language and Poetry

The CW collect provided for Mothering Sunday is a prayer for healing, rooted in a relative clause that draws together Jesus' childhood in Nazareth and his death on the cross. It is both complicated in the theological connections it makes and not easily related to the thanksgiving that many will bring to church on that day. Certainly, Mothering Sunday is a day when prayer for healing and comfort is particularly important—but 'The Gathering' may not be the time for this.

However, though we are arguing for a smaller set of collects and simpler echoes with the place in which people stand before God, this is not necessarily a demand for language that is stripped of its poetic richness. Indeed, with a smaller set of collects that have the chance of becoming familiar, quite the opposite is true.

The need for cleaner theological connections between salvation history and the here-and-now is about easing the movement of the liturgy. It is not an argument for dumbed-down language. Why not rich it up? It is often the case that poetic allusion, rhythm, resonance and insight is stripped from the church's worship for the sake of those who live where deprivation is high—but this only serves to deprive more.

Collects for Different Contexts

Whilst a primary focus of the collect is the transition from Gathering to hearing the Word of God in Communion, there are other contexts, times and places in which they may also be used: at baptisms, confirmations, weddings, and funerals (where the liturgical role is similar to the eucharistic context); and in Services of the Word (where, for instance, the collect might be placed just before The Dismissal). CW provides a specific collect each for the first four of these but there is no specific provision for A Service of the Word.

As each of the festivals is quite different this remair a valuable side-dish to go with the staple diet

If attention were directed to just 7–10 seasonal collects, each of which would act as a sort of girding prayer for key transitions in the liturgy, it may be that the need for prayers which work equally well in different parts of an act of worship could be accommodated.

The other provision made by CW is a corpus of collects to be used with the Festivals and holy days of the Christian Year. As each of the festivals is quite different this remains a valuable side-dish to go with the staple diet. Here also is some of the theological stretching that can be dipped into from time to time and which will enrich the year for those who follow the church's pattern of daily prayer.

Putting it All Together

We fully acknowledge the strong and pressing arguments for a set of collects for each Sunday and festival of the year, in a very different style from those provided in Common Worship. What we have suggested, however, is a different approach to the whole question of collect provision. It is one that would mark a change for the Church of England, but it has connections with some previous and current practice. We believe that the genie of diversity of collect use is now well and truly out of the bottle, and will not be put back in. No-one is suggesting that any new set of collects would *replace* those in Common Worship—they would, rather, be an alternative 'package.' Why not then, offer a third alternative: the seasonal approach that we have suggested here. Again, there is precedent in the Anglican Communion. *A New Zealand Prayer Book* (1989)[19] provides three collects for each Sunday and festival, of different styles and lengths, and the decision as to which is used is a local decision.

This is our suggestion for the future:

- For *starters*: collects for each of the 'occasional offices,' pitched at the needs and expectations of the congregations that gather for those services, most of whom are occasional visitors to church rather than regular worshippers;

- As a *side-dish*: collects for each of the Festivals and Holy Days, which can provide some variety and theological richness for those who require it;

- And as a *main course*: perhaps somewhere between seven and ten collects, (one for each of the main seasons and maybe four for the long summer/autumn period of Ordinary Time) which fulfil the need for prayer at liturgical transition points, whether that be from Gathering to Liturgy of the Word in Communion, or, say, from Prayers to Dismissal at other services. These would be in *addition* to full sets of Sunday collects (the Common Worship set and the new set from the Liturgical Commission), which could be used in contexts in which they were appropriate.

A Step Further—Opening Up To The Extemporary

The form of daily prayer often known as *'The Durham Office'*[20] uses this 'Opening Prayer':

> Blessed are you, Christ our Lord,
> our everlasting light
> and redeemer of the world.
> *[A few lines of extempore prayer may be added here.]*
> By taking upon yourself our mortal nature
> you saved humanity
> and restored joy to the whole world.

The use of extemporary prayer is a means of drawing the here-and-now into the liturgy, which is often overlooked in the Church of England and should, perhaps, be pursued further. It may be that formal liturgies would require the caveat found in Hippolytus' Eucharistic Prayer *'providing it is orthodox'*[21] but this would be a small price to pay for the prize of such freedom.

Perhaps the same approach could be taken to collects as is already taken to the lectionary in Common Worship, by providing 'open' and 'closed' seasons? Common Worship provides for locally devised, or locally selected, lectionary provision to be used outside the strongly seasonal parts of the year.[22] *New Patterns for Worship* provides over forty such 'lectionary modules,' but these are not the only options.[23] During the strongly seasonal parts of the year a fixed seasonal collect could be provided, or the Common Worship set of collects (or the new alternative set) used. Outside this 'closed' season, the choice of collect could be made more open, or a series of collect forms could be provided which incorporate the option for flexible insertions. These 'insertions' might fit the theme of a service, the reading to be preached on, or the particular situation of the local congregation (such as the recent death of a key member or the opening of a new church building). They could be either extemporary in the strictest sense (made up on the spot) or prepared beforehand but locally devised. We have provided examples of the sort of thing we have in mind in the final chapter.

Some Sample Collects

5

The collects suggested here are drawn and adapted primarily from the Common Worship set. This is on the basis that there is little point looking further afield if there is usable material already available—and when you are looking for a small number of collects it is possible to find them within CW. The samples here are intended primarily to illustrate the approach that we are suggesting, rather than to provide a definitive set of collects. Unlike the CW collects, we have printed each prayer with a 'short' ending as the 'default' (except in cases where the Trinitarian ending is intrinsic to the way the prayer is written). A longer Trinitarian ending could be added as appropriate.

Collects for the Seasons

Advent
Holy God,
give us grace to cast away the works of darkness
and to put on the armour of light,
that on the last day,
when Jesus shall come again in his glorious majesty
to judge the living and the dead,
we may rise to the life immortal.
[through the same Jesus Christ our Lord.]

*CW First Sunday of Advent, abridged and altered
(including changing the address from 'Almighty God…')*

Christmas
Almighty God,
in the birth of your Son
you have poured on us the new light of your incarnate Word,
and shown us the fullness of your love:
help us to walk in his light and dwell in his love
that we may know the fullness of his joy;
who is alive and reigns with you,
in the unity of the Holy Spirit,
one God, now and for ever.

CW Second Sunday of Christmas

23

Epiphany

God of life and light,
in Christ you make all things new:
transform the poverty of our nature by the riches of your grace,
and in the renewal of our lives
make known your heavenly glory;
through Jesus Christ your Son our Lord.

CW Second Sunday of Epiphany, with altered address

Lent

Almighty God,
whose Son Jesus Christ was tempted as we are, yet without sin:
give us grace to discipline ourselves
in obedience to your Spirit;
and, as you know our weakness,
so may we know your power to save;
through Jesus Christ your Son our Lord.

CW First Sunday of Lent,
with reference to Jesus' forty days in the desert removed

Easter

Lord of all life and power,
who through the mighty resurrection of your Son
overcame the old order of sin and death
to make all things new in him:
grant that we, being dead to sin
and alive to you in Jesus Christ,
may reign with him in glory;
[to whom with you and the Holy Spirit
be praise and honour, glory and might,
now and in all eternity].

CW Easter Day

'Pre-Advent' (All Saints' to Christ the King)

Almighty and everlasting God,
you have kindled the flame of love
in the hearts of your people who have gone before us;
grant to us the same faith and power of love,
that, as we rejoice in their triumphs,
we may also be sustained by their example and fellowship;
through Christ our Lord.

CW Fourth Sunday before Advent, altered

Collects for Ordinary Time

Because there is no 'seasonal focus' or theme for these Sundays, the collects need to be general enough to serve on any Sunday of the period, as well as being appropriate to serve as prayers that work at transition points in the liturgy.

Ordinary Time before Lent

Loving God,
by whose grace alone we are accepted and called to your service:
strengthen us by your Holy Spirit
and make us worthy of our calling;
through Jesus Christ your Son our Lord.

CW Fifth Sunday before Lent, with address altered

Ordinary Time after Trinity Sunday

Almighty God,
whose only Son has opened for us
a new and living way into your presence:
give us pure hearts and steadfast wills,
to worship you in spirit and in truth;
through Jesus Christ your Son our Lord.

CW Fourteenth Sunday after Trinity

Creator God,
you have made us for yourself,
and our hearts are restless till they find their rest in you:
pour your love into our hearts and draw us to yourself,
and so bring us at last to your heavenly city
where we shall see you face to face;
through Jesus Christ your Son our Lord.

CW Seventeenth Sunday after Trinity with address altered

Almighty and everlasting God,
increase in us your gift of faith
that, forsaking what lies behind
and reaching out to all that lies ahead,
we may run the race before us
and win the crown of everlasting joy;
through Jesus Christ your Son our Lord.

CW Eighteenth Sunday after Trinity, altered

Some 'Generic' Collects

These collects provide for extemporary (or pre-planned, but locally determined) insertions. They could be suitable either for seasonal time (in which case the extemporary part might naturally relate to the season) or for ordinary time (in which case the insertion might relate to the readings, theme, nature of the service or some other particular aspect of the day or worship).

A Generic Example with Extemporary Petition

Almighty and everlasting God,
you are always more ready to hear than we to pray
and to give more than either we desire or deserve:
*[here a request appropriate to the day, readings, theme, season or situation is
added]*
We ask this through Jesus Christ our Lord.

CW Twelfth Sunday after Trinity, with provision for extemporary prayer

A Generic Form with Extemporary Section Relating to God's Nature Suitable for Use Near the Beginning of a Service

God,
whose nature is...*[here reference is made to some specific aspect of God's
character, nature or action]*
help us whose nature is not fully fit for heaven
to hear your word,
draw close to you in worship
and hold our world before you in prayer;
through Jesus Christ our Lord.

A Generic Form with Extemporary Section Relating to God's Nature Suitable for the Latter Part of a Service

God,
whose nature is...*[here reference is made to some specific aspect of God's
character, nature or action]*
help us whose nature is not fully fit for heaven
to respond continually to your word,
remain bound to your will
and hold our world before you;
through Jesus Christ our Lord.

Notes

1   Martin R Dudley, *The Collect in Anglican Liturgy: Texts and Sources 1549-1989* (Alcuin Club Collection No 72, Liturgical Press, Collegeville, 1994) p 5.

2   An examination of his collects from this and a devotional standpoint is to be found in C Frederick Barbee and Paul F M Zahl, *The Collects of Thomas Cranmer* (Eerdmans, Grand Rapids, 1999). See also L Stephens-Hodge, *The Collects: An Introduction and Exposition* (Hodder & Stoughton Prayer Book Commentaries, 1961).

3   P Akehurst and A Bishop, *Collects with the New Lectionary* (Grove Books, Bramcote, 1972 and three further editions).

4   *News of Liturgy*, No 324, Dec 2001.

5   First published in hardback in 1997 as *Opening Prayers: Scripture-related Collects for Years A, B and C from The Sacramentary.*

6   ASB Rules to Order the Service, Rule 1a.

7   ASB Rules to Order the Service, Rule 9.

8   ASB General Notes, Note 7.

9   ASB Rules to Order the Service, Rule 1b.

10 Note 2 on p 375 in the Common Worship main volume.

11 Note 3 on p 375 in the Common Worship main volume.

12 Commentary in *Calendar, Lectionary and Collects*, p 249f.

13 Commentary in *Calendar, Lectionary and Collects*, p 250.

14 Commentary in *Calendar, Lectionary and Collects*. p 250.

15 *Common Worship: Daily Prayer*, pp 310–313.

16 *Opening Prayers: Scripture-related Collects for Years A, B and C from The Sacramentary* (Canterbury Press, 1997)—the ICEL collects.

17 First published by Canterbury Press in 1997 as *Opening Prayers: Scripture-related Collects for Years A, B and C from The Sacramentary*

18 *A Prayer Book for Australia* (Broughton Books, 1995).

19 *A New Zealand Prayer Book: He Karakia Mihinare o Aotearoa* (Collins, 1989)

20 Published initially as *Daily Prayer* (a series of booklets) by the Durham Diocesan Liturgical Committee in 1998 and now available in book form: Bruce Carlin and Tom Jamieson (compilers), *Daily Prayer: a form of praise and prayer for use at any time of day* (DLT, 2002).

21 See, for instance, Geoffrey Cuming *Hippolytus: A text for students* (Grove Liturgical Study No 8, 1976) p 14.

22 See the Common Worship main volume, note 7 on p 540 and note 5 on p 27. The implications of these notes are spelt out more clearly in *New Patterns for Worship*, to be published by CHP in autumn 2002.

23 To be published by CHP in autumn 2002.